Beyond the
CUTTING EDGE

A collection of medical poems by

Dr. Naaz Jahan Shaikh

INKQUILLS®
FOR THE READERS, BY THE WRITERS

Published by InkQuills Publishing House

www.inkquills.in

First Edition 2025

ISBN: 978-81-982215-3-7

To all those who hold a scalpel in the hand

One thing we must never fail to understand

A scar we create both, on the body and mind

Cut only if necessary, and never forget to be very very kind!!!

This book is dedicated to my parents,

Late Mr A.M. Shaikh and Late Mrs. Sakinabi Shaikh

My love, light and inspiration

About The Poet

Meet Dr Naaz Jahan Shaikh, a surgeon-poet whose poetry collection unveils a profound confluence of healing hands and lyrical heartbeats.

In the operating theatre, her craft is guided by the sharp edge of science, wielding steady hands to heal bodies. Beyond the sterile field, however, she crafts verses that illuminate the emotional contours of the human experience.

This collection invites readers into the dual world of Dr Naaz, where each poem mirrors the delicate balance of a surgeon's existence - a place where life, loss, and recovery unfold with raw beauty.

Her verses pulse with the rhythm of clinical reality, capturing the weight of decisions made in seconds and the lingering truths carried long after the gloves come off. In her hands, medicine becomes metaphor, and poetry becomes precision, every line a thread that connects science to spirit, flesh to feeling, and mortality to meaning.

Dr Naaz Shaikh's journey reminds us that the art of healing does not stop at the body. Through this intricate fusion of practice and poetry, she extends a hand not just to mend, but to reveal the profound humanity in all who seek solace, survival, and hope.

Incisions and Insights:

Beyond the Cutting Edge

"Beyond the Cutting Edge" is a compelling collection of poems that traverse the delicate intersection of science, healing, and human emotion. The cutting edge - a symbol of precision and advancement - represents the tools of a surgeon's trade and the boundaries of modern medicine.

But this collection goes beyond the tangible edge, delving into the uncharted realms where surgical precision meets the unspoken truths of life, loss, and resilience. The title evokes a journey beyond the mechanics of the scalpel and into the profound experiences that lie beneath- where every incision carries not just skill, but a story.

"Beyond the Cutting Edge" invites readers to step into the dual world of a surgeon-poet, exploring the complexities of healing bodies while grappling with the fragility of the human condition. These verses, like surgical threads, weave together emotions of triumph, vulnerability, and endurance - offering a refuge of understanding for those willing to step into this realm of depth and discovery.

May every reader find solace, insight, and a renewed appreciation for the art of healing, both within and beyond the cutting edge.

Wishing all the readers, a pleasant submersion!!!

About The Cover Page

"Beyond the Cutting Edge" by Dr Naaz Jahan Shaikh beautifully captures the essence of vintage medical literature while intertwining the art and precision of surgery with thoughtful reflection.

The deep navy and brown hues, enhanced by golden flecks, evoke a sense of an aged masterpiece reminiscent of classic medical texts. The faded handwritten script in the background enriches the design with nostalgia, hinting at the memorable personal stories and experiences inscribed in every surgeon's mind.

The gold accents symbolize moments of discovery and enlightenment, perfectly aligning with the book's exploration of transcending conventional limits.

Central to the design is an intricately patterned scalpel, emphasizing the artistry involved in surgical practice and a reminiscent of the craftsmanship found in historical instruments. The sharp, angular typography of the Cutting Edge conveys surgical precision, while the golden carvings reflect the gratifying victories in the healing process.

Overall, this cover is a masterful fusion of vintage medical aesthetics and contemporary poetic insight, inviting readers to delve into its profound themes.

Acknowledgement

First and foremost, I am profoundly grateful to my family and friends, whose gentle whispers and unwavering nudges guided my pen through the labyrinth of emotions.

I extend my heartfelt thanks to my husband, Saliya Dharmayath, for his steadfast advocacy and patient listening.

The beautiful cover design was brought to life by my daughter, Aarzoo, and son, Aamir, whose artistic touch and boundless creativity made this book visually captivating.

I am deeply indebted to Dr C.S Rajan who instilled in me a love for words, knowledge, and the power of expression. Your wisdom shaped my journey as both a student and a lifelong learner.

To my teachers, colleagues and fellow surgeons, who inspire with their precision, dedication, and compassion.

To all my patients, your stories, insights, and shared moments have enriched these pages in more ways than one.

A special note of gratitude to the entire team at InkQuills Publishing House, who skillfully guided me through this journey from manuscript to publication with care and expertise.

And to you, dear reader, thank you for picking up this book. I hope these poems find a place in your heart and resonate with your experiences and reflections.

With immense gratitude,
Dr. Naaz Jahan Shaikh

Foreword

"Medicine is a science of uncertainty and an art of probability"
said Sir William Osler.

The book "***Beyond the Cutting Edge***" by Dr Naaz Jahan Shaikh, uses a good mix of the uncertainties and probabilities of the surgeon's life, powered by the use of rhyming verse, to give a gripping reader interphase. It is not an easy book to put down, and offers a good relaxation, to all levels of the medical field, more so, to her fellow surgical colleagues. It will be a treasured copy in the book collections of all doctors.

It is a privilege to be invited
To write the foreword of any book on Surgery,
But to be requested to do so for this treasure,
'Beyond the Cutting Edge', written in verse,
Is an Honour and an immense pleasure!

My own first encounter of medical verse was in 1970s time
The reading of 'The Diagnosis of the Acute Abdomen in Rhyme'
Written by Zachary Cope under the pen name of 'Zeta'
To describe the Pandora's Box's pathological games fiesta,
As played out in 1949.
This book fascinated me in the poetic style,
Of information transfer using words versatile,
To give meaning to the acute abdomen dynamic
Prompting easy clinical diagnosis and treatment frenetic.

Move ahead by 70 years, and today, we have our own Dr Naaz
Putting medical and surgical thought, with intervention,
Into meaning, by use of the poem
That gives the peruser much reading satisfaction.
The book's title infers the work to be extracurricular,
As reflections of fact and event flow,
After the patients have been seen and treated.
And, of surgical tools that are oft not remembered.

The period of experience crosses the dark days of Covid
The troubles of which Dr Naaz has written so vivid.

The narrative is distributed to make reading compelling
And topics blend into the next, with smooth flowing.
With each subject having the complete pack,
Of introduction, substance and an end, with a message hack.
The construction remains uniform in both sections,
'Medverse' and 'Coviverse', giving an easy recitation.
The illustrations are few but apt to script interactions.

The book has a universal appeal, across all levels
Of the surgical ladder, from young medicals
Through post-graduation, young and senior surgeons,
To the armchair, retired persons.
Offering the unique blend of information, light humour,
Intrigue, and a final 'take home' for the consumer.

I strongly recommend this book, penned with zest
As I wish Dr Naaz Jahan Shaikh, the very best.

Dr. C S Rajan
Emeritus Consultant Surgeon, Bengaluru.

PART 1 - MEDVERSE

PART 2 - COVIVERSE

MEDVERSE
PART 1

Poetry in Medicine

Poetry in medicine is often unseen
Give us a page and give us a scene
To narrate what, when and how it has been
And publish the same to let us be seen.

Expressing in verse is no less a talent
To put all in place we need to lament
Bringing together the fragments of thought…
The signs and symptoms must also be sought.

We need to add a soft and soothing touch…
To feel the pain, imagination you must stretch
The lines must reach the bottom of the reader's heart
Striking the right string is no less than an art!!

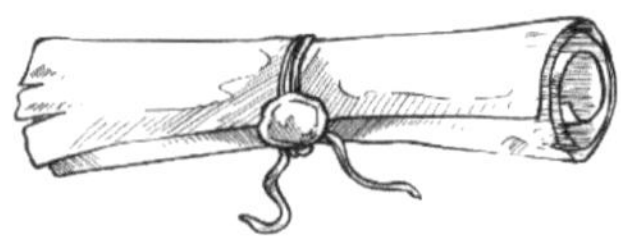

Zeal to Heal

Waking up from my slumber sweet
Cutting short my dreams, I retreat
Burning oil all the night
None to lend a hand, none to hear my plight!

Sacrifices I've made every day
Yet, time and again I have to prove my say.
When all is well, I am their deity
My place is next to God Almighty!

Shouldering a huge basket full of stress
Healing the sick from distress.
The tick of a clock clearly heard,
The small hours of the night spent, unspoken, unheard.

A bad patient, an awkward disease,
An imperfect decision in a tricky situation,
Abruptly changed now, is my position
All at once, I cease to stand in the crease!!

Abuses I hear,
Assaults I bear,
Yet, when the next of the sick arrive

I strive, to let them survive.

Is this all I deserve?

For the sacrifices I made, just to serve.

All the while I stood on my heel,

Only 'cause, I had the zeal to heal!!

Shaikh, N.J. Zeal to Heal. Indian J Surg 81, 609 (2019). https://doi.org/10.1007/s12262-018-01860-6!!

Every Wound Tells a Story

Every wound tells a story
When you gently probe into the history.
Thermal or mechanical trauma may be the cause
The host could give a clue, for a moment, pause.

Is it Skin deep or reaching the bone,
And Slough within or microbes borne
Smell it and sense the foul odour
And assess the discharge for its colour.

The surroundings mean so much more
Oedema and erythema could increase the sore
Timely, think of the right covering
To protect it from the microbes hovering.

If dry, use something moist and soft
If infected, use the local nano crystalline shot
While hydrogels could hydrate and keep it wet
Alginates and foams absorb the fluid that is let.

A gamut of skin substitutes, help to heal
Ranging from the skin allograft to the potato peel
Be it a pressure sore or a diabetic ulcer

Need a different approach altogether.

Negative pressure could come in handy
To make the profuse discharge, fairly scanty
Smart dressings will come to the rescue
And dictate the treatment plan for me and you.

Alleviate the pain and reduce the misery
The child within is pleading, with eyes, watery.
The escalating costs could punch a hole
All said, never fail to see the patient as a whole!!

The Humble Scalpel

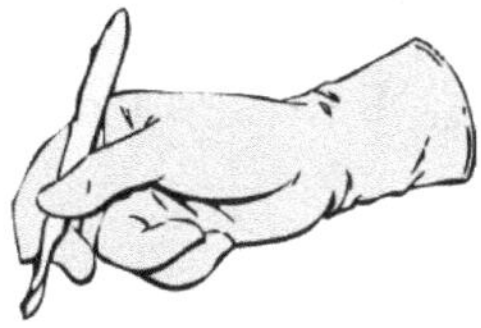

Surgeon has a power so very unique
He cuts and heals with a magical mystique.
His power is doubled with a scalpel in hand
The decision to operate comes with experience, we understand.

A surgical knife has a history interesting indeed…
Evolving from shells, leaves, bamboos, fingernails and shark teeth.
The Neolithic cutting edges made of flint, jade and obsidian
Could incise precisely, including the skin and the bone.

Metal slowly replaced the rock and stone
Efficiency improved with copper, bronze and iron
Hippocrates named it Macairion,
And, the Romans called it Scalpellus.

Varieties emerged in its make and design
From double edged (catlins), to fixed or foldin'.
Ambroise Pare and Chaulic preferred it to be very ornamental
But carbolic acid and heat to these were detrimental.

Then came the era of disposable blade with a handle reusable
Gillette with their safety razors became instantly sensational.

When blade exchange and fixing was irksome
Bard and Parker's design was indeed awesome.

Studs replaced the ribs for a better blade hold
Stainless steel handle could now withstand the heat and cold.
With new arrivals they had a hashtag (#) and a number
But they had no major features that we had to remember.

The cutting edge was made more sharper and stronger
With Addition of zirconium, diamond and a coating of polymer.
But evidence today confirms the fact
Neolithic obsidian blades had a sharper impact.

Technology has added many a shade
Even, current passing can induce a heated blade
A high frequency vibration can cut and coagulate
And, the cyber-knife can precisely incise and modulate.

To all those who hold a scalpel in the hand
One thing we must never fail to understand
A scar we create both, on the site and mind
Cut only if necessary, and never forget to be very, very kind!!

When The Bag Is In Trouble

That pear-shaped bag,
Lying humbly under the liver crag
Performing till date the duty allotted
Until the time its contents got tainted.

Precipitation of the sludge
Stones at times resembling fudge
Silent often... but sometimes yell
Their untold story they seem to tell.

The undefiable 'F' sequence
Now and then have given credence
When Murphy's sign gives a clue
It is time now to inform the crew.

The situation is grim with a triad of Charcot
Worsened further with a pentad of Reynold
Intervention is needed to clear the yellow,
Needed at times is the help of an expert fellow.

Acoustics and the magnets will guide you
Knowledge of the anatomy will always take you through
Hug me says the gall bladder,

Lest you put the pivotal trunk in danger!!

COSIC, will ease the situation

Rouviere's sulcus, is a prominent demarcation.

Without a critical View of safety, never clip under tension

Sometimes, doing less is better than a stupid temptation!

Ignorance of the miss is worse than committing

Safe conversion is always worth attempting!!

Shaikh, N.J. Poetry in Medicine. Indian J Surg 80, 297 (2018). https://doi.org/10.1007/s12262-017-1697-9.

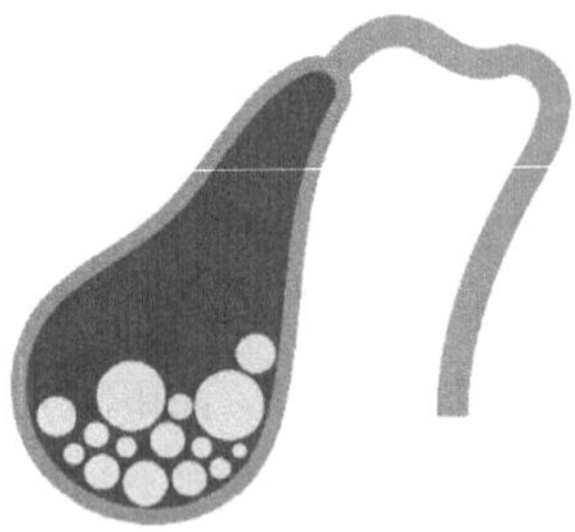

Jewel's Betrayal

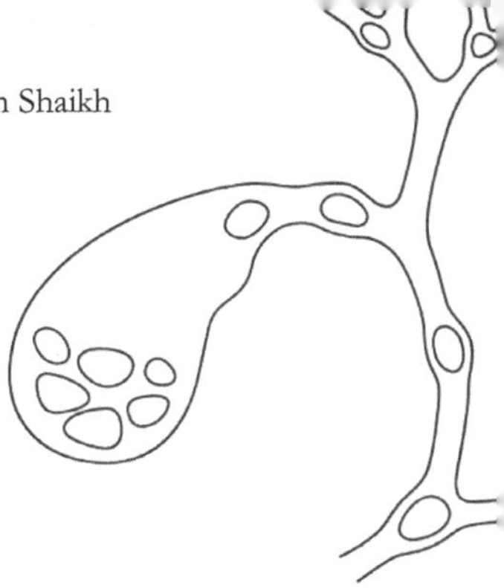

I donned my ethereal Phrygian cap
And clutched my cherished Hartmann pouch
Gently displacing those jewels I gathered
Feeling proud of my unique collection
Faceting each other harmoniously
Wanting to stay together, to exhibit
Their collective super power!!

Until that day when, one jewel missed its directive
Gently passing beyond the limits, demarcated
Went ahead to reach my neck, slender and narrow
Little realising it caused a serious problem!!

Now I had swollen from head to toe
Tense and tender, turned fat and globular!
Blushing more than I usually did
Felt so helpless under the liver, where I hid.
Minute after minute beginning to feel worse
My cap and pouch, with me in toto
Losing my identity as I lost my battle!!

Time had come to say goodbye
To all the organs who lived nearby.

Slowly, as I began to be separated

My jewels inside were getting disintegrated.

Now, as I depart I realised,

That, the jewels I had accumulated

Stealthily, got me subjugated!!

The Meandering Path

All was well until one fine day
When the crypt shut itself out of the way
Slowly and steadily, it began to swell
Infection in the potential spaces started to dwell.

The contents of the closed tight space
Caused throbbing pain, reducing the pace.
When the tension could no longer be held
It burst open, to relieve the contents gelled.

No doubt, this relieved the pain
But the track caused problem again an' again
The new path caused so much misery
As pus kept leaking from its territory.

Mostly caused by infection non specific
Rarely by Crohn's, Cancer an' Tuberculosis.
The track had an opening one within
And, one or more over the skin.

Seeing the outer by easy perianal inspection
And inner, by digital dimple palpation.
A Sonography or MRI could delineate the wall

But the surgeon's finger was the master of all.

The study of its course was of prime importance
To determine the complex path, needed patience.
To estimate the depth, high or low,
Perform the procedure, steady and slow.

The time was now ripe to operate
And the team was all set to cooperate.
Procedures to be understood were so many
Each had its drawback, that was the irony!

Lay the low open, along its course
For a rapid healing, without much resource.
Difficult to treat was the fistula so high
'Cause it had the anorectal sphincter in the nigh.

A lesser procedure is to disrupt the tract
A glue or a plug could have a similar impact
Perform the LIFT, when in need,
A Fistuloscope is another gift indeed.

When in doubt, seton takes the chance
Tight or loose, healing it does enhance.

Misery of the patient we cannot measure

Cosmesis and continence could be a boon of laser.

Sepsis could cause that troublesome gap

Which needs to be covered by a vascularized flap.

Cutting of the sphincter does not really matter

Unless, enough is left, to circumvent the bitter!!

Shaikh, N.J. The Meandering Path. Indian J Surg 82, 751 (2020). https://doi.org/10.1007/s12262-019-02039-3

The Ampoule of Lies

Lies in our lives are meant to hurt
Annoying everyone, as the venom they spurt.
But there seem to be exceptions to this rule
As I often proudly hold a lie filled ampoule.

Seeing a man whose limb is black like a charcoal
I assure him success, sans his body as a whole.
The terminally ill patient with a deadly cancer
Partly closed eyes, and life around in a shatter.

His hands I gently hold with distress
A lie I whisper, while a tear I suppress.
As I handover the new-born in the hands of the father
While, gasping on the bed lies the mother.
Though often I know that we cannot conquer
Never I hesitate, so many lies I utter.

Knowing very well that a heart that fills the chest
Has lost its power to pump at its best.
I bring a smile false, to my lips
And express that it's time to start enjoying life's sips
Death, I understand, is the greatest reliever
And time undoubtedly the greatest healer.

Yet, I fight with God Almighty every day

And never hesitate to fill my bowl with lies on my way.

This bundle of lies I carry along

Marching forward with this extra prong

But the weight of these lies seems to be so light!

'Cause I know I have lied, to relieve someone's plight!!

Ref: Under the Green Leaf by Dr Naaz Jahan Shaikh, InkQuills Publishing House

An Ode to Trauma Care

In the eyes of trauma all are one
Young or old, rich or poor, it spares none.
A collision head on, or a trivial fall
A hit with a missile or a cricket ball.

Timely arrival of a medical team
Will calm down many a scary scream.
Trained staff with their wit and skill
Prevent the deadly bleed and the chill.

Following ABCDE is a must
In every step you lay your trust
In the golden hour you must enable
And make the patient fully stable.

Skillful handling of the mass casualty,
With that minimum available facility,
With a proper trauma triage
Many a life you can salvage.

A basic assessment with a FAST
Will guide you along, super-fast
Look into the patient's eyes!

For, the pupils offer many signs.

Turn them around like a log of wood
A look at the back is a must and should.
Bleeding takes the first priority
And, Damage control takes the superiority.

Reassessment is the rule
To investigate, make use of available tool.
The team strives day and night
Each member is no less than a knight.

Each one walks that extra mile
To retrieve the patient's lost smile
The healer thanks almighty for the battle just won
As the injured walks towards home on his own!!

That Lump In The Breast

(A poem on breast cancer)

A symbol of beauty and the grace of motherhood
The little ones suckled more often than they could.
Changes so frequent from menarche to menopause
The scene each time deserved umpteen awes!

When the study of pathology came in handy
The changes understood were due to ANDI
A deviation from the norm could be confusing often,
The lump which had formed, sent a wave of tension!!

The fear of cancer crept into the mind,
A phase of denial pulled the string from behind.
The visit to a doctor was so very late,
Now the curse had shifted on to fate!!

A battery of tests, were performed in a sequence
Every test was best at its performance.
A mammo and a sono complimented each other.
With a needle test the diagnosis was not farther.

The tests revealed the lump was benign,
Yet a suspicion suggested not everything was fine!!

An excision biopsy would solve the mystery
A benign report would signal a victory.

But luck seemed to have lost its way...
The journey seemed to move on a sleigh!!
Time was locked behind the doors,
And, happiness exhausted all its stores!

The time had come to plan the therapy,
Which was undoubtedly a multi-modality.
That terrible feel under the knife...!
And the chemo added more to the strife!!

A 'Radio' further compounded the mayhem
Life had to slow down which was at its helm!
Sympathy was not what was expected,
Rather, a supporting shoulder to lean the head.

With the Damocles' sword hanging overhead
So difficult it seemed now to move ahead.
Courage and confidence were the tricks of the trade.
Life seemed beautiful on getting back it's shade.

Faith in the almighty and trust in the healer

Will cure the disease which is such a killer!!

Every day lived, now seemed like a bonus…

To gather strength and overcome the clonus!!

A lesson learnt is worth very sharing,

Early detection has a very good bearing.

A few minutes spent each day to replenish the balance ....

Would undoubtedly add miles and smiles to the life's substance!!

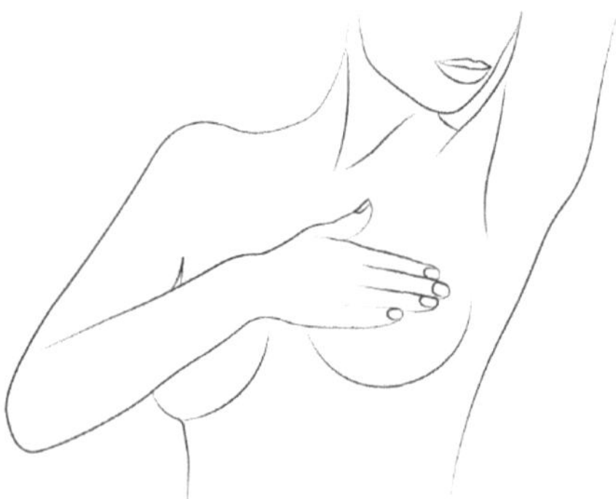

Unveiling The Pandora's Box

The magic wand I held in my hand
And unleashed the mystery as I slowly scanned
Every organ seemed to talk,
Holding some sign towards me they walk!

The play boy bunny seemed to wink,
And the humble IVC collapsed into the 'sink'.
The night seemed bright with a starry sky,
But all was not well with icterus in the eye!

That bright ball could be a venous ball,
The target in my mind I could not miss at all!
Was it a wheel within a wheel or the bull's eye...?
And the water bags, signalled the parasite.

The tombs of bacteria within the gall bladder
Were the cause of pain, which seemed to bother.
Was it a SIN or a WES, I couldn't miss...
If failed to pick, it would lead to a mess.

Were the Kidneys in their original place?
Or had taken a tour to the other ways
The twinkle behind that little star

Pointed to the cause of pain so far.

Was it a ball or a bean? that was yet to be seen,
To know the lesion, I got very keen.
The spokes of the wheel beckoned the lesion was benign,
But a calcification in the fat said all was not fine!

Fascinating it was to see the colour...
On both sides there was a fire in the bladder!
When a pocket was seen attached to the wall...
The prostate then, must take a call.

The aperistaltic tube that was blind
Hiding often somewhere behind
More fluid within, implied a danger
Obstruction by the 'lith' would cause it to rupture!

A ring of fire down in the pelvis
Caused by the pregnancy in the wrong place.
The whirlpool sign of the twisted pedicle,
The dermoid was deceptive like the tip of the iceberg!

The womb failed its duty of nature,
When the tiny balls within changed its stature.

The ovaries seemed kissing each other...

The idea of the chocolate didn't please either!

The Aorta seemed standing tall

Thank almighty! Pepsi symbol was not to be seen at all!

Slowly and steadily I now mowed the lawn

The gut gave its signature and the final line was drawn!!

Shaikh, N.J. Unveiling The Pandora's Box. Indian J Surg 82, 1324 (2020). https://doi.org/10.1007/s12262-020-02197-9

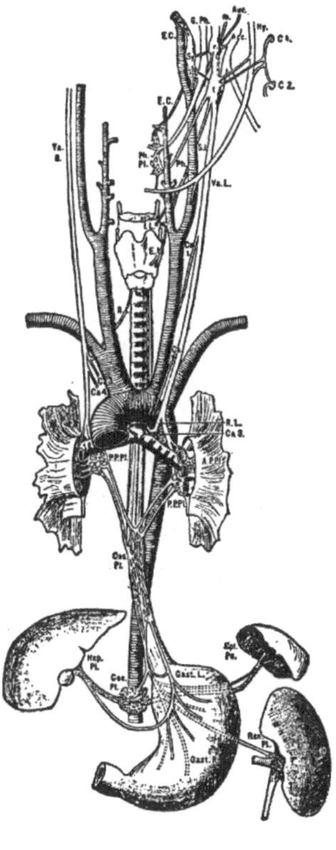

When The Cell Stops Listening

I am a cell, the unit of all life
In everything alive you can find me in rife.
I align myself as a building block
To perform my functions, with my neighbour I lock.

In animals you can find me minus a cell wall
In a unicellular, alone I do the functions all.
You may find me working as a little prokaryote
Or the more organized bigger being, the eukaryote.

My information centre is the nucleus,
In which I hide my genetic make which is so inconspicuous.
Outside which is the fluid called the cytoplasm...
Where I harbor certain roadways, the endoplasmic reticulum.

My energy house is in the mitochondria
And proteins modified in the Golgi's atria.
My life is controlled with a lysosome…
My division is limited and purposeful, aided by the centrosome.

My cycle has check points to show my limitation
My life has to end, mortal I am, I have my substitution!
My relationship with the host is a perfect symbiosis

When my role is over I program my end through apoptosis.

When my core is hit once, I still keep my calm.

When hit twice I pledge now to cause the harm.

I break myself from the reins of the immune system

Sometimes send my army in disguise to a remote destination.

My nutrient needs are no longer dependent.

'Cause through neo-vascularisation, I have now become independent.

Catch me and curb me if you can when it is very early

Longer the delay you will miss the bus, certainly.

To kill me now, the right weapon you must choose

And all the cruelty on me you must let loose.

With my illogical behaviour I jeopardise my host..

And I fail to understand that this loss is my loss too!!

When The Going Gets Tough

(A poem on constipation)

When the going gets tough...
Even excessive pressure is never enough
There certainly overlies a gloom
That day for the patient is without a bloom!!

When it happens once in a way
With a laxative you can do it away.
But when the trouble is frequent
It is time now to lament.

Digging deeper into the history
Diet and habit, reveal the mystery
Rule out that hidden stricture…
Which may at times be benign or a cancer.

IBS, creeping with a problem also in the mind,
Use Rome criteria to differentiate the kind
When the transit through is dead slow...
Colonic inertia is something you must know.

Failure to relax the pelvic floor
Which at times acts like a trap door

Descent some times of this diaphragm
Needs to be studied on a skiagram.

Stimulate the bowel or increase the bulk
That would prevent many a sulk.
A change in the habit may do the trick
And soften the stool which was as hard as a brick!!

The Muddle of Appendicitis

Abdominal pain of any kind
Keep appendicitis also in mind.
When the clinical score is very high
The facial appearance is also wry.
When your fingers don't unleash the mystery
Peep again into the history.
With an ultrasound you can see
What your fingers sometimes failed to feel.

Focus where the "Target" is
A watchful eye will pick with ease.
Appearance of secondary features
Will guide you of the next procedure.

The baseline diameter as a six
Look for signs that affix
When more fluid is seen inside
Urgency must be on your stride.

Echogenic fat in the rim
Or a free fluid at the brim
A ring of fire on the doppler
Among the sonologists is very popular.

Then comes the C.T scan
Judiciously use, whenever you can
Caecal bar sign or the enhancing pic
Diagnosis is available on a click.

Moments of delay will punch a hole
When in doubt peep through the keyhole,
Act wise, act fast and blow your mast...
With a prudent decision you will surpass!!

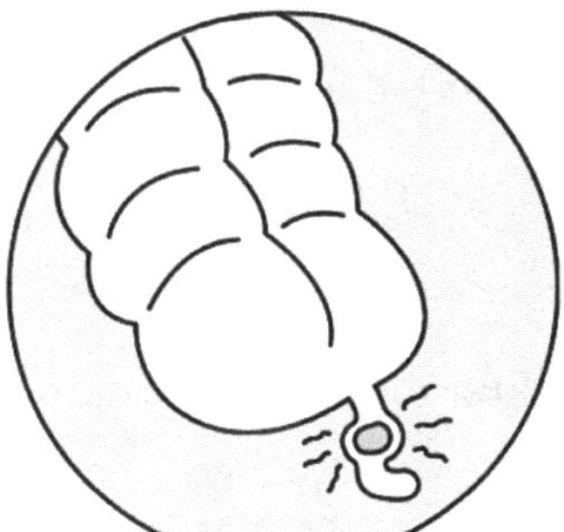

A Victim of Deceit

A slender, cute little appendix
Resting on its cosy, warm bed
Draped by its mesentery, dancing gracefully...
Tickling everyone, playfully.

Reacting often to the happenings around
Yet, trying to cope with the hostile ground
Frequently, sympathizing with the ileum
Sharing its problems, maintaining equilibrium.

A soft chat with its friend, the blind caecum
Caressing the ovaries and the rectum
Wanting not to carry any worries along
Waiting to rest and hum the chorus song.

But luck wanted it otherwise ...
When the cunning ileum pushed across
A stone, that blocked the spirit of happiness
And began to hurt with its nastiness.

With a false promise to do no harm
Rested the stone, pretending to charm.
A disturbed milieu intensified by its silence

While tears began to flow in abundance.

It was time now to save the kith and kin
Though deceptive, ileum had to stay within
And the caecum was engulfed in sadness
As the two lovely friends parted their ways.

Now, lying in its grave in a remote pathology lab
Blaming the ileum for the cruel back stab.
Waiting to prove his innocence he struggles
Generations come and go, the matter never settles!!

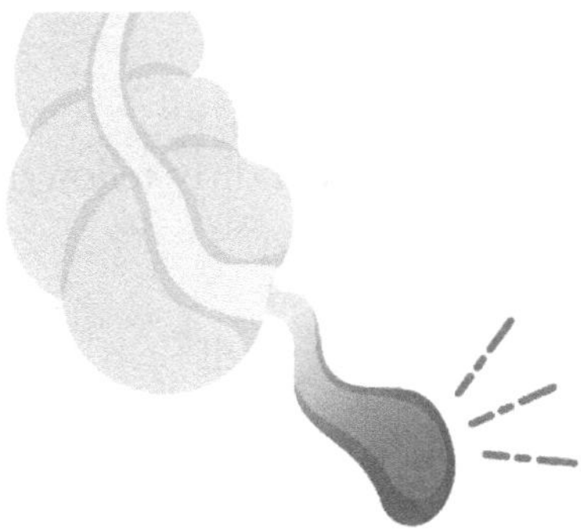

The Mysterious Lith

Where do you come from
And where do you want to go?
Who puts you in and ...
Why do you want to make a show???

Middle of the night or in the broad daylight
With anyone anywhere you pick up a fight.
You are the cause of the roll and the plight
Look around, is there any help in sight?!

You are seen hiding in the biliary bag
Slipping down at times in the biliary tract.
Changing the hue to a dark yellow
Why should you not be labelled a dirty fellow?!

You jam the appendix and let it swell
Some deep trouble is now what we smell!!
Down in the colon you form those pellets
Getting the going tough is what you result.

As the clearance in the kidneys has been messed
Your presence in an odd place has distressed.
The agony you cause is so very serious

To get you out is painful and laborious.

Seen sometime in the umbilicus
And, not uncommon, in the pancreas,
Name some place and there you are found,
Not to miss, under the tongue, you hide underground!!

You seem to be in various shapes and sizes,
In each location your presence surprises.
You could be the invisible microlith.
Or the lithopaedion, seen like a monolith.

If I could only get to know ...
Who put you in and how did you grow?
I would pick you up and make that throw
And prevent you from making the deadly show!!

The Lost Arch

With the sugars steadily surging
The limb victimised, silently crying
Its perspiration lost and so was sensation
The disappearing pulse, added to its frustration.

A flattened arch, and toes like sausage
Lustreless dorsum and a tough, hardened sole
The limp now was prominent and salient
All of them signalled, a danger was imminent.

With a pressure distribution so improper
A painless foot added to the disaster
Abundant sugar, a milieu loved by invaders.
With infection superadded, the body quietly suffers.

The microbes went on digging deeper and deeper
The bone wasn't spared of this damage, either
A crater so deep wouldn't agree to heal
Demanding expert's intervention with utmost zeal.

The foot assessed and a footwear designed
Pressure distributed, to an area wide.
The inflow assessed and blocks cleared

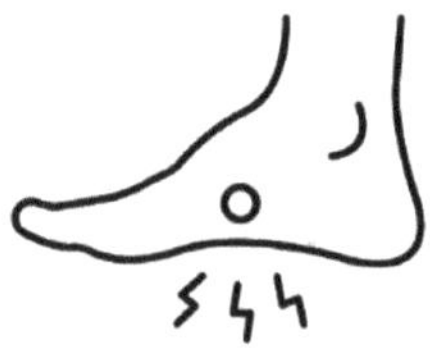

The body as a whole got the attention it deserved.

With luck hiding behind a mysterious door
The foot could no longer be set on the floor
A decision to sacrifice, had to be made
During an amputation, wept the surgeon's blade.

Time to revive the carelessly lost treasure
With a good control of sugar, and an eye on measure
Just akin to a stitch in time, often saves nine,
If the arch is maintained, the limb could be fine!!

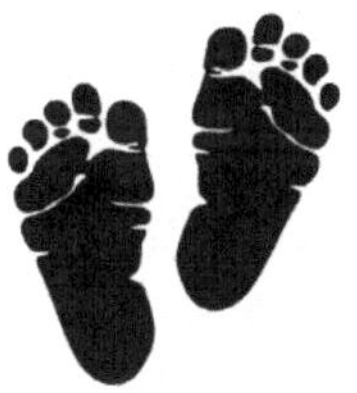

A Tiny Little Zygote Who Lost Its Way!!

My journey I began as a tiny little zygote
Travelling along, dreaming to be a beautiful little neonate!!
Crossing all the hurdles placed in my path
Rolling and twisting in the roller coaster track.

My journey somehow got delayed
As the road I travelled was a little bit ragged.
That deceptive bend which I had to tend
Was actually a complete blind end!!

In a frenzy move I was caught in a whirl pool
It seemed now, I was so much like a fool
I couldn't negotiate any longer
As my size now was much more bigger!!

My resources were limited
My destination had changed
Forced I was, to cut short my journey
Before the situation to my host, turned very stormy!!

Discussed frequently as a topic
As I had chosen to be an ectopic.
My end now was so very certain

My role had ended, down was the curtain!!

Alas, I was so short sighted!!
My whole purpose was defeated!
A careless move took my toll,
Me with the track were destroyed as a whole!!

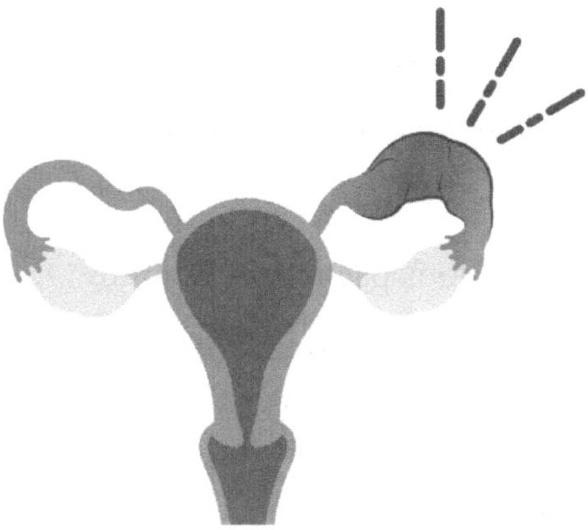

Ectogenesis- A Boon, or a Bane??

Sitting in my room all cosy
I came upon the news that took me to a frenzy
An environment created to match with nature
And babies born sans the womb of the mother!!

With an egg donated and preserved
Fertilization was so far in vitro
Be it as a donor of the egg
Or, someone who wanted to be the surrogate!

Emotions and sensations packed to the brim
Love flowed on seeing the unborn foetus swim!!
Now, we bypass the environment of the uterus
That stood testimony to the growth of the foetus.

It carries hope for a couple that is gay
Or someone who would avoid a surrogate
A woman engrossed in building her career
Or a disease that damaged the womb so severe.

No more Cesarean sections to blame the doctor
And preventing a mother from dying was another factor.
The cost was something one would worry

And many more factors to make us feel sorry.

With babies cultured in the lab
Values and emotions pushed under the slab
Could this come as a blessing in disguise
Or will it make humans pay a heavy price???

Time bears testimony to all the doings
But, bypassing nature could someday bring ruins!!

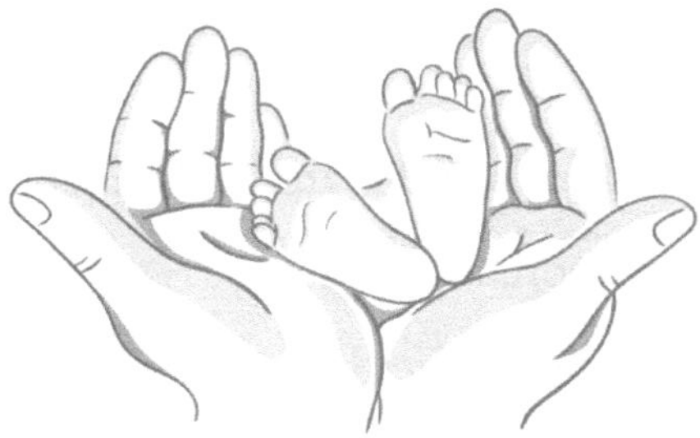

The Mysterious Linear Ulcer

The mysterious linear ulcer
I am told is the enigmatic fissure
And when it occurs aboral ...
The pain experienced is unimaginable!!

Acute, when its duration is less than six weeks
And exceeding beyond, it would now be chronic.
The hardening of contents passing through
Is the main cause we can construe.

Childbirth sometimes can also be the culprit
Now and then, Crohn's and TB are on the pulpit!!
Occurs posteriorly more frequently
Ischaemia is said to be the factor behind this.

When acute, ease the pain with a stool softener
Analgesics would do the function of a pain eraser.
The chronic needs a treatment much harsher
Choose the right treatment and inform the sufferer.

Sphincter relaxant with a shot of Botox
And a high fibre diet would do the detox.
Surgical treatment for sphincter release

Will bring the lost smile back on the patient's lips.

Do it right to relieve the sphincter so tight
A little too much, adds incontinence to the patient's plight!!
Choosing the right treatment is always an art
Undoubtedly, you would see a smiling patient now depart!!

The Lub And The Dub

The two were twins non identical
The tiny little lub, and the larger mighty dub
Playing hide and seek in synchrony
Far far away from the world's cacophony.

Their play was indeed very well organized
The game starting at the SA node on the right side
They moved along the path fixed for them
Maintained the discipline which showed in their rhythm.

All was fine and the heart was happy
Until one day a misunderstanding threw a floppy.
Something seriously was wrong at the node
Creating a chaos in their safe abode.

The rhythm altered and so was the game
Neither lub nor dub took the blame
At times as slow like the tortoise's beat
Sometimes as fast as an athletes feet.

There was the time when brady came in
At times displaced by the tachy plungin'
They heeded to the intruders an' gave in to mischief

Awe struck; the heart missed a beat in disbelief.

The tachy game took it's turn
The V tach and the AF both caused the burn.
The paroxysmal tachy, still holding on to rhythm
It's beginning and end none could fathom.

As the rhythm suddenly seemed out of reach
A mighty shock with a defib came to beseech
When the time to travel seemed to be long
A pacemaker came in as a companion for life long!!

Both Lub and Dub seemed disturbed forever
Scared to be buried under the weight of fat and sugar,
With folded hands, knelt down, in humble prayers
Begged for fitness, to continue as players.

Journey of a Mop to Gossypiboma

Once upon a time I was a mop
White as ivory, turned into a sop
In I would go and clean the muck
And in the process somewhere I got stuck.

Lying inside creating no harm
Enjoying thoroughly, the milieu that was warm.
But the body wouldn't want to accommodate,
Every attempt it made to destroy, to ablate.

Stubborn I was, wouldn't budge from my place
Silence, I thought was the mantra of solace.
Slowly and steadily, I built my cocoon
The body now, could never impugn.

The grass on the other side appeared greener
And my desire to see the world grew stronger
Eroding slowly into a loop of bowel
Creating a barrier as I entered this tunnel.

But, nature somehow could not accept
An intruder somewhere, I became a suspect
Pushed across the CT table, I could no longer hide

I was picked by the tag on me, that was my honour, my pride!!

Back in the OR, there was an operation search

Quickly, I was pulled out and laid on the table

Fearing the fate of the previous healer

I prayed to Almighty to be his saviour!!

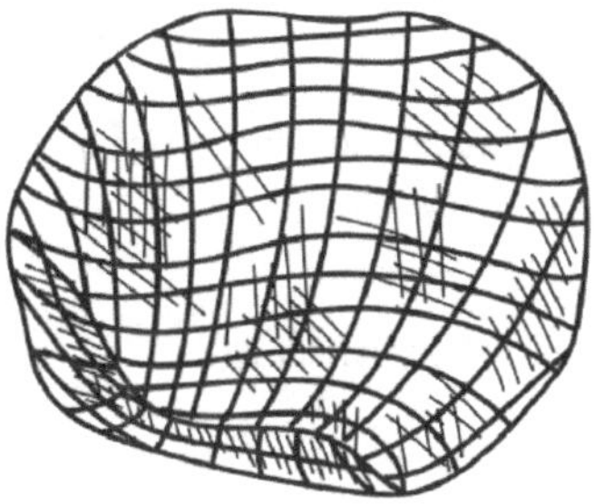

The Hernia We See

That defect in the abdominal wall
Let go the contents, which now begin to fall
An innocent looking bulge at a very wrong place
Is a cause of misery and a frown in the face.

Tactfully and gently, it was possible to reduce
Until one day it failed and was a cause for abuse.
The saga of pain and swelling was now very frequent
It was time now to see an expert to close the rent!!

One by one, the curtain began to fall
An AWR surgeon could now see it all.
A sono and a C.T did show the defect
An MRI would also be very perfect.

The size of the defect was to be assessed
And the loss of domain was not to be missed.
That non anatomic fold seen at last...
Was a reminder of the prosthesis used in the past.

An IPOM, a TAR, a Scola or a MILOS ...may be selected
And a TAPP or a TEP/E-TEP... based on expertise results are expected.

Between onlay, inlay and a sublay one must choose
To decide, put your feet in the patient's shoes!!

A defect too large is a challenge for all
Even an expert's confidence may at times fall.
A fasciotens comes along to our rescue
Never mind the cost, if you've decided to subdue.

To do the best, choose the right mesh
Synthetic, dual or biological, every case is a fresh.
To Handle with utmost care, is the rule
If infected you will feel, worse than a fool!!

Learn the components of the abdominal wall…
A thorough study of anatomy, must be understood by all.
Tailor a procedure for every different situation
And that will lead you to a right destination!!

In Need Of A Burp...!!

I was a little bubble of air,
Happily running, rolling and riding
Every time the tongue was in motion
I ducked and created a sensation.

As my confidence grew taller
I leaned on the tonsillar pillar
And mocked at the tongue
'Cause it could not harm, until so long.

My game was all over
When I was pushed by a large bolus
Into a very steep terrain
And I had no chance to refrain.

I stumbled and tumbled
Only to reach a pungent cave.
Unable to bear the stench so acidic
Every minute passed; I felt so terrific!

Looking for the exit I bumped into the antrum.
Who gently pushed the pylorus open.
So kind enough, he gave me a ride

And showed me how and where to slide.

My ego by now had to invariably soften.
Looking down, it dawned, this was only an entry
And the exit was far away leading to another boundary
My relief had only a short history.

My exit there would again be forbidden.
Where, time and place would be of utmost concern.
I pulled myself back and looked for a solution
To take a shortest route was my intention!!

In desperation, I kneeled down and bowed my head
And only Almighty could help, they said.
At last, my prayers were answered
A burp came to my rescue, before my hopes were shattered!!

Quickly, it lifted me and climbed up its way
From trouble, it advised me to stay away.
And as I was pushed with a soft mumble
My ego had gone, and that made me humble.

As I slowly walked out happily into the open
I thanked Burp for the love and affection it had shown!!

The Cu-T Sans The Copper

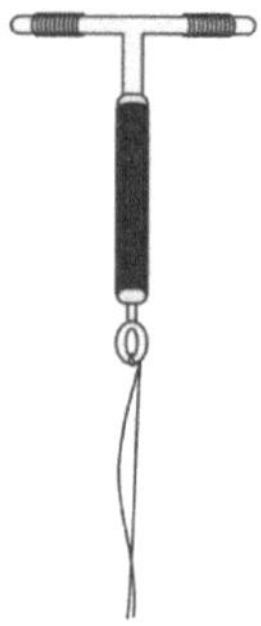

Sneaking through a gap by my side
I saw this sperm wriggling towards
The tiny ostium of the fallopian tube
In search of the ovum, to quickly fertilize.

I had failed my job, as I stayed longer
A milieu hostile, wasn't so any more.
Marching forward was an army of hope
I pitied the ovum, wondered how she would cope.

A tough choice she had to make, it did seem so
Exiting the ovary, as she squeezed her torso
Ready to embrace hope with all delight
A dilemma of selection, that was her plight.

The job was done and she began to swell
She marched towards the womb, a place to dwell
But was caught in the strait, as she grew oversize
And had to settle there, without a second choice.

Blamed for the failure, I would be kicked out
If left longer I would have migrated, no doubt
A precious life could no longer grow within

I silently slipped out, to save my skin!!

Greening the OR

Greening the OR is the need of the hour
Environmental protection is the duty of one and all
Let pollution be a focus at your every step
Lest you convert mother earth into an unworthy steppe.

The OR generates revenue for me and you
And abundant waste which is hazardous too.
Patient safety is always the first priority
Keep in touch with the recycling authority.

Gadgets used must be disposed and reprocessed
The cost reduction must also be assessed
Collection and segregation must be a rule
Appropriate funds you must pool.

Reusable linen reduces a major burden
Custom kits to be used only now and then.
Power saving is also needed to sustain,
Proper lights with a lesser energy is a must to brighten.

Waste gases must be scavenged
The laws of the OR must never be contravened.
The gas flows must be timely checked

Leaks if found must be contained.

Temperature settings to reduce interference,
Patient comfort is always given major preference.
Make the roof a source of energy generator
Or a green roof to act as your sole protector!!

Proper Waste disposal in containers appropriate
With the help of this you most segregate.
Environmental care is our responsibility
How well we do, exposes our unique ability!!

The Paradox of Positive

Swimming in my mother's womb
That warmth and grace I could feel
Yet she seemed so aggrieved
Sobbing and crying, feeling deceived.

The truth slowly unveiled
She was 'Positive' for the dreaded disease!
Her innocence cleaved and shattered
The man she trusted was a beast in disguise!

Left abandoned in this cruel world
Snarls and abuses towards her were hurled
She had a choice to end her life
Or let me live to face the strife.

My innocence abruptly came to an end
As I realised everybody would pretend
My presence unwanted and my words unpleasant
My disease was the cause of their dissent!

A different school where me and another
Shared my story and hence wouldn't bother
Looking at the world around me that was so cruel

I had to live my life which at the start had a bevel.

Used so often by people who hoodwink

I loathe their presence as they stink

The legacy unwanted I was presented with

Why does the world encourage such a myth!!

Someone Somewhere Becomes a Doctor

Someone somewhere choses a profession
Vigour and ego traded for sacred compassion
Hearing someone's plight was more important
Curing the sick was the motto and determinant.
A choice was made by a little child then
Like the soldiers who decide to serve the country men.

The definition of thrill changed all of a sudden
And the gurgle of the bowel answered with a sound forbidden.
The inflow and outflow that was silently changing
And the lub and dub now had a different meaning.

Stones here and there began to create interest
A specialty chosen in every different context.
Halitosis wasn't at all displeasing anymore
As a tube was thrust into the windpipe to blow oxygen and more.

Looking into the eyes was no more romantic
More interesting was to peep deeper into the mystic.
Ears were looked as some kind of caves
Where mystery hid behind the sound waves.

Some got glued to screens creating a documentary

Suspense unveiled as history became complimentary
Those clever eyes struck a chord deep within
A gentle music played as a ball of diagnosis began to spin.

No one realised, when there was a change in thrill
And the mind walked to soothe that cry so shrill.
Not all can choose the profession that could involve
A commitment of a lifetime and the family's resolve.

A Surgeon's Step Ladder

Experience has taught me many a lesson
Leaving in mind a permanent impression.
At every indication I was eager to operate
But time has taught me when not to operate.

Sword is mighty, but mightier is the scalpel
Treating hands, more divine than the folded hands in the chapel.
Put in all your thoughts before you cut...
Remember, invasion is only the last resort.

A proper history you must take
Never ignore this, for God's sake!
A peep into the patient's past
Would give you that important clue at last.

A Personal and the family history
Would reveal many a mysterious story
Habits always leave a trail
Look for signals needed for a smooth sail.

A thorough clinical examination is the rule
Ignoring this will prove you a fool
Prudently choosing the right investigation

Certainly, would ease many a tension.

When in doubt examine again
For, many a sign appear often very late.
Internal examinations you must do
To save your skin from much ado.

Choose a pen or the scalpel,
When necessary to look in, never delay.
Needed sometimes is an opinion poll
Which will drastically reduce a disaster toll.

Never miss to take the consent,
This requirement you must never circumvent.
Let your path lead along the checklist
Lest you forget something during that unexpected twist.

To stay ahead, you must stay updated
The society would otherwise think you are outdated.
The secret of success lies with the team
With collective efforts you can fulfil your dream.

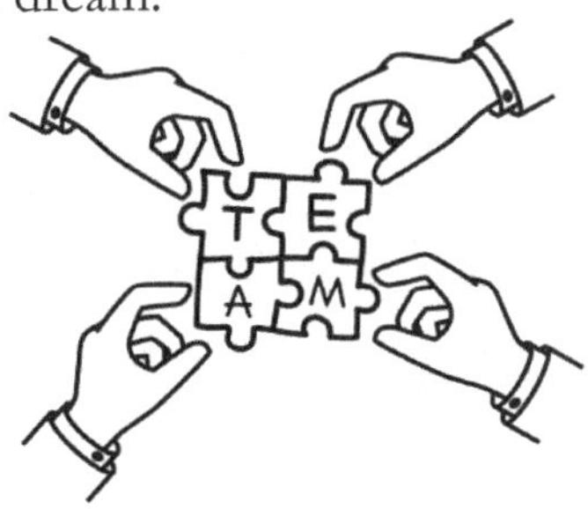

Plight Of A General Surgeon

Scalpel in the hand,
And a Healing Skill in the mind
Surgeons they are
A noble breed of a different kind.

Saviours of the yester year
No less a battle like the mighty soldier.
Bringing back that lost smile
Name any ailment from the scalp to the Pile

Moves of his are so meticulous,
Working hours though endless,
Smile he carries, hides all exhaustion,
'Cause his profession is his only passion.

The mighty scalpel is no more sharp
Losing its shine slowly in the time warp
Old now was new just yesterday
Things he did have just faded away.

Situation today is so hapless
Seeing more and more of less and less
Dividing the patient bit by bit,

The Surgeon general today, has lost his grit.

Society so diverse and the laws so hard
Some get so much and others nothing at all.
Patient suffers, and so the surgeon too
Empowering the surgeon is all we need to do.

Give him the power and enrich his skill
Mastering the art, sooner he will.
Boost the confidence with a pat on his back
And bring the scalpel holding surgeon general, back on the track!!

A Feeble Cry From The Womb

Happy I was in my mother's womb,
Unaware of the times to come
Clinging to the umbilical cord,
Like a pea in its pod.

Swimming in the limited space,
Feeling the warmth of my mother's grace
Little suspecting my gender would be
The cause of my cruel end!

Scanned I was,
Whispers I heard,
That I would be meeting,
My end, sooner or later.

Wondered I, 'bout the cause,
Days to come, the truth unveiled,
I would be thrown into a pit,
The female gender was the culprit!

Woman gives birth, she is the mother
She is the sister, the aunt and the grandmother.
Above all, she is the beloved wife,

But the daughter to come is always unwelcome.

My mother cried to save me,
But stubborn were all around,
When the healer was the killer,
It hurt me like I was stabbed with a tiller!

Every time the womb was firm,
I writhed inside with pain.
The time had come to leave the womb,
Much before the end of term.

Feeling weak wondered I,
What could be worse?
With no daughters to come,
How could there be wives and mothers?

Ref: Under the Green Leaf by Dr Naaz Jahan Shaikh, InkQuills Publishing House

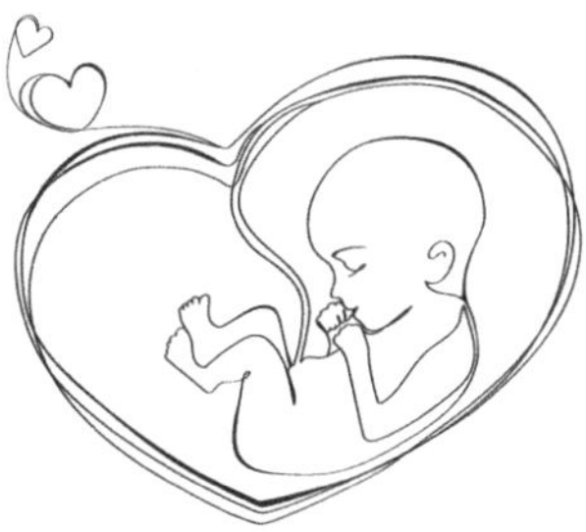

COVIVERSE
PART 2

The Unseen Enemy

Where did you come from, where do you wish to go
A widespread devastation you've caused, don't you think so?
The world is in agony, as it is slowly dismembered
The disaster struck, that will long be remembered

The world's business has come to a grinding halt
With markets shut the countries are bankrupt
Little children imprisoned with a fear lurking,
Over their heads the Damocles' sword is dangling.

A kin lost, and another on the verge of dying
Agony of not saying good bye gives a painful sting.
With dead bodies to be buried piled in the waiting
The silence around is so chilling, so appalling!!

What makes you so audacious, so vicious
Sans a cell you take mine and make it fictitious
Mercilessly disease my body, you are utterly glossed
Please stop this cruel act, before hope is lost.

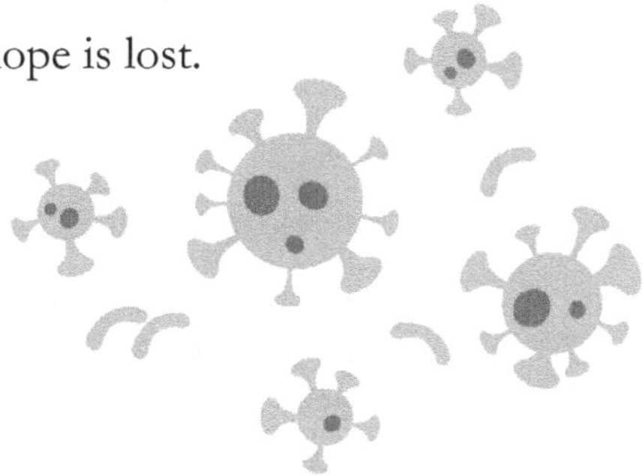

Bask With a Mask

I am very tiny, yet so cardinal
My role today has been phenomenal
From controlling the spread to a bare minimum
I can save lives, if my use is optimum.

Keep me handy and use me always,
To keep yourself safe from the demon in disguise
Take me along, even with a friend on a pillion ride
The virus doesn't differentiate, it doesn't hide.

Made of cloth, or scientifically layered
Choose the right at the place appropriate
To stop the shower of the virus around
Cover your face and nose, keep it properly bound.

Though a tiny piece, today my worth is priceless
My premature disposal would drop you lifeless.
Take utmost care and stop the temptation to cluster
Your life is precious, and only you can add a lustre.

Heed to science, and listen to the scholars
Never ignore, keep track of the rising numbers.
Anger and anguish are not the answer to the plight

Lend a helping hand, to at least the nearest in sight.

Never let down or loosen your guard, at any time
Roaming around unmasked is indeed a crime!!

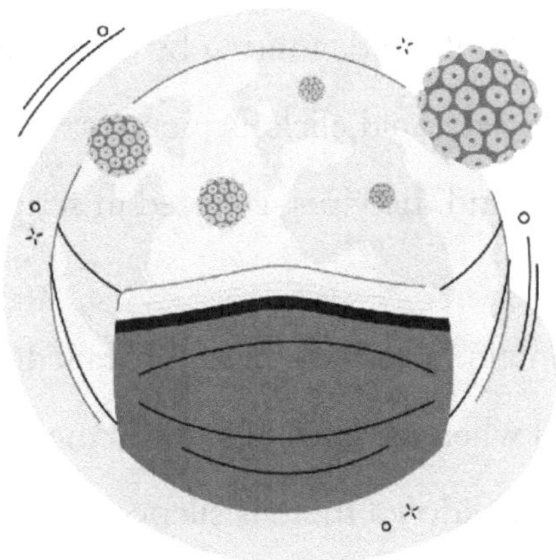

Caught Between Numbers

Caught between numbers rising every second
To look normal, each of us tries to pretend
Panic in the air as Corona creates history
What made it to surface is a total mystery.

Was it a biological war experiment gone wrong?
Or unhealthy and unkind devouring by mankind?
Science so advanced could click its pictures
With a crown around the virus, is noted in scriptures.

Measures to contain its spread miserably failed
Panic multiplied when newsfeed by social media misled
With world in a lockdown there is silence around
The fear for life is the cause for this astound.

Reserves depleted; markets abandoned
With no means for transport, travellers stranded
Health care working overtime seems to be burdened
Improper personal hygiene is a cause for concern.

With schools shut and exams cancelled
We realise that health takes priority, for once!
But yet it is ignored most, as kids are burdened

With lots to learn, play and recreation ignored.

We talk of weapons to fight across borders
And research directed towards disaster survival
Less attention is paid in building a strong human
We are fighters by birth, is oft forgotten.

Gifted we are with an immune system
Designed to fight during every invasion
We care more for science than for nature
But the two are inseparable, yet of a different measure.

Let's get back to the basic teachings
Good personal hygiene must be within our bearings
With simple measures let's wipe away this misery
Conquer the disease and prevent replication of history.

Death, I Wish... You Could Come Some Other Time!!

(The thoughts of a cover 19 sufferer on ventilator)

Caught intricately between the wands of time,
Preoccupied, I had been all these years, very fine,
With no time to spend I was a miser
A new dawn did not give any pleasure either.

Time was money, and I was always eager
To earn much more, I wandered hither and thither.
My outward appearance was so different
Stunned was the inner me, seeing me so stringent.

Hungry for applauds I was mounting the ladder
Fame had blunted my senses forever.
Now I have realised, there's very little time left
I want to come, for death would leave all bereft.

Distance seemed so difficult to travel
The obstacles in the mind failed to unravel.
Now when my breathing is difficult, I realise
Me being forgotten, even before my body dries.

As the world today has come to a stand still

I wish to talk to my kin and explain my will.
My fame, my wealth didn't matter even a little
But a morsel of food and a kind word did.

My final journey would be royal I dreamt,
But death, you do not hear anybody's plight!
You come at your will and leave silently
And when asked to wait, disregard blatantly.

I want to talk to my children and run around
To capture moments of happiness floating abound.
I wish you could come when I am ready
I do not care a little when I sound so greedy.

Listen to my request and step back a mile
I will rectify myself and come back in a while.
The time now is a painfully difficult trial
There's none to accompany me at my burial.

Come to me when I am with my kith and kin
After they have pardoned me for all my sin.
Take me away when the time is sublime
My only wish is you could come some other time!!

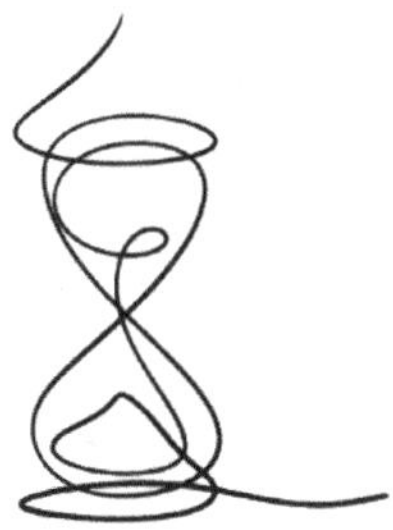

2020… A Year That Wasn't!

A brew of happiness in every glass
Splashing gently with every cheer
Screams of joy lit the roads and lanes
As we welcomed the new year with open arms.

Disaster was waiting around the corner
Struck this world with a silent yet heavy hammer
Shattered were the dreams of every dreamer
Clutched their lives, hiding from the silent killer.

Distancing became an accepted norm
Yet the souls craved for a hug so warm
Kin lost, departed without a royal march
And the bodies wrapped were left to parch.

Hunger killed someone around the corner
Yet the corrupt hands never stopped to devour
Sacrifices of warriors often fell on deaf ears
Who served unconditionally without any fears.

Santa waits with his bag now empty
As his shelf the whole year did not get a bounty.
With fear still lurking in every mind, is inhibiting

To open the arms and welcome a new beginning.

A ray of hope from someone somewhere
Can kindle a desire to live and survive
With a positive thought let us embrace
And brighten the coming year!!

Once Bitten and Twice Shy

Once bitten and twice shy
I hesitate to embrace, I don't know why
The new year is just waiting round the corner
And my eyes wouldn't want to look yonder.

Fear bottled within my heart holds me back
A fear of losing a life and a fear of failure
In times so difficult my mind slowly withers
Waiting for blessings in the form of strong feathers.

Prayers and wishes fulfil my dreams
And slowly I stretch my arms to feel
Positivity brings a change immense
As I slowly accept the challenge and commence.

Let me be the light that lights
The hopes of many, and reduce their plights
A soothing word or a helping hand
To pull the needy from time's quicksand.

Like the Santa so selfless and understanding
I will distribute love and joy, that is so rewarding.

No Good Byes, No Farewells

No good bye, and no tears of farewell
The journey begins for a new place to dwell
With no hands to hold and comfort through
The path of transition, unknown to me and you.

Reduced to a person, name transformed to a number
Adding to the list of oxygen hunger, is another member
Gasping for air, every breath so heavy and difficult
A shortage creates a fear, heralding death is near.

Often, we hear that the families entirely vanished
Each couldn't see the other, though in distress
The departed souls craved for a final adieu
The belongings that lie scattered, wondered why.

Wealth accumulated never came to rescue
But a good deed and a helping hand did.
Ego got buried under the carpet of distress
Equally affected were both, from a hut or a fortress.

We are all so tiny in the hands of the mighty destiny
Like a bubble on water, our lives, waiting to be blown in a jiffy
Hold on, and stretch the strings of love and kindness

Together we can overcome this raging tempest.

The Deafening Silence

(Kenopsia)

Where is the crowd, where are the people?
That mad rush of people engulfed by a gripple
The road is deserted and so are the holy places
Fear is seen lurking on people's faces.

The school is silent and the playgrounds empty
The swing simply squeaks in memory of aplenty
The green grass eagerly waits to be mowed
The fountain with a loss of vigour has slowly bowed.

The people seem to feel the silence so deafening
And the situation of the present so demeaning.
Depressing was the thought of monetary loss
But the fear for life seemed like betting on a toss.

A difficult time though, this too shall pass
Distance from the society for a while it demands
A blessing in disguise for mankind indeed
A family time, a peep within, is today's need.

As The World Heals

Taken aback, traumatized by the oblivion
As the world was struck by the Contagion
The world seemed to come to a grinding halt
Dreams dampened, unable to bear the assault.

Newer grounds converted into burials of the masses
When lives lost akin to a falling row of dominoes
More prayers were heard in places of cheers
And, caretakers of health emerged as new heroes.

Confused were animals to see humans in cages
The air seemed cleaner, as respired by the sages.
The world will continue irrespective of who left
And once again life will go on without any bereft.

Lamenting about the happenings so far
It implies, God has a plan, He has left his door ajar!
Taking this opportunity, the earth has begun to heal
Back on the shore are rare fishes, including the seal.

The animals in the forest are back on their feet
As the ugly eyes no longer follow them on the street.
Remarkable is serenity and happiness in their eyes

Each animal cares for the other without any malice.

I pray to the Almighty that let this harmony prevail
My new World I wish, is like Eden of Adam and Eve's.
Where life is more valued than specious luxuries
And personalities will be remembered for centuries.

Unpolluted streams and air around are unmodified
The lush green forests, homing innumerable birds.
Their musical chirp emanating in such synchrony
More spectacular than Beethoven's symphony.

Shunning all technology that hurts our fellow being
I would build a nest, incorporate love and caring
Share happiness to multiply and grow exponentially
Let humanity, reverence and kindness prevail eternally!!

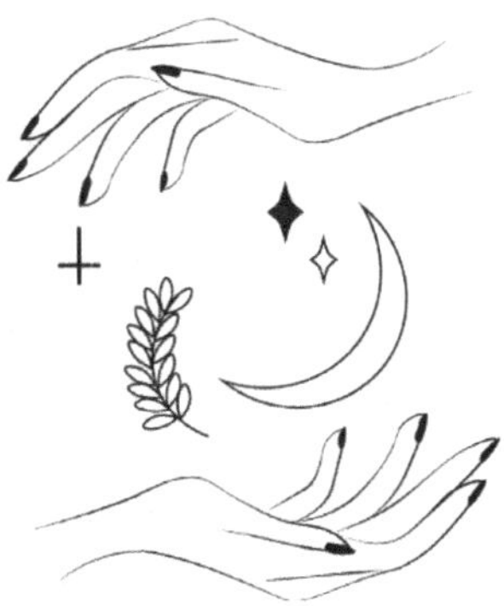

A Humble Prayer

A turmoil I see all around me
The fear for life lurks in every eye I see
The apprehension of losing the kin, is deep within
A frustration surfaces when survival chance is thin.

Death scares the young and the old alike
A little more time is what each one would like
The luxuries locked behind every magnificent door
The needs are reduced to a square meal for the four.

Animals wonder what has conquered mankind
With cruelty diminished, only love is left behind.
Every minute passes with so much uncertainty
A new dawn, brings a sigh of relief in conformity.

The wait for normalcy seems so very endless
A prayer is chanted when life becomes seamless.
With eyes closed, let's feel closer to Almighty
And sense his power within, with or without a deity.

With Holy books, holy thoughts and a pure heart
Solace, harmony and prosperity they will impart.
My humble prayers to ease the pain in the world

Our creator listens, patience is the way forward.

Is This What a (Covid) Warrior Deserves??

Fighting relentlessly to ward off the unseen enemy
Pulling back from a scene, the dying so many…
Tired and weak, yet we continue to treat
Ignoring hunger, and tossing away even a call to sleep.

Covid warriors in white coat, we emerge as a team
Surviving on meagre supplies, yet carry a lot of hope.
Infection lurking around, would catch us too, no doubt.
Your life is our priority, to save you, we fight.

Unarmed often, brushing aside a thought that it is suicidal.
A refusal to prepare or even serve food, furthermore.
Suffering an infection doesn't bother so much
But, with serendipitous violence we are bewildered.

Beaten at times or even humiliated to the core!!
God forbid, when life is lost serving the diseased
There is none to pay a homage nor to accompany
The final journey seems so scary, so lonely!!

Refusal to even grant some space to be buried
It Hurts!! A plight, must not happen even to the worst enemy.
Claps and burning lamps are valued least

False appreciation hurts as people turn into beasts.

When a warrior in a battlefield loses a life
The Country stands up mourning for the martyr
Lauded with praises, and a chorus of applauds
Respectfully laid, with prayers to rest in peace.

But frontline warriors against the corona battle
Starve for supplies for safety and survival.
A humble request to the nation and its people
A respect they deserve, and a place in reserve...

That place of burial, without any controversy
And a load of respect during the final journey!!

(Based on violence/ atrocity against covid warriors in India)